Supercharge Your Love Vibe

The Supercharge Your Love Vibe Training Course

The inner-world system for your outer-world success.

The scientifically based inner secrets of how I prepared for the man of my dreams & learned to love again – and how you can too!

BY ELIZABETH MENZEL

Book 3 of the Supercharge Your Vibe! series

DISCLAIMER

The material contained in this book was developed from the personal & professional experiences of the author, Elizabeth Menzel. Ms. Menzel is not a mental health professional and makes no claim to be one. She does not make any diagnoses, and she makes no claims to be able to do so.

This book is not intended as a substitute for the advice of and treatment by a qualified physical or mental health professional. The publisher and author are not responsible for any adverse consequences or experiences that may result from the use of the ideas, perspectives, and/or tools discussed in this book.

If you proceed to read and use the material contained in this book, you are accepting responsibility for your actions and the results you create. If you have questions about the efficacy and utility of this material for you, we advise you to consult a health professional or other qualified advisor before implementing the ideas shared here.

DEDICATION

This book is dedicated to you who know what it's like to feel so heartbroken you don't think you'll ever be able to scrape yourself off of the floor, worry that your heart might be frozen forever, or have given your all and gotten little in return. It's time to align yourself with the vast love of the Universe and see what it's like on the other side of a fully open healthy flowing heart. Give this gift to yourself and as you supercharge your love vibe, help others to supercharge theirs.

ALSO BY ELIZABETH MENZEL

Supercharge Your Health Vibe!

WOMEN'S HEALTH BEST-SELLER

Get ready to learn my favorite ways I keep my energy strong all day long, feel healthy even when I'm sick or injured, and how I learned to love my body and become the healthiest me I can be, so that you can do the same for yourself.

Supercharge Your Money Vibe!

WOMEN'S HEALTH BEST-SELLER

Get ready to learn the exact ways I quadrupled my financial income by changing my poverty consciousness to prosperity consciousness as well as how I improved my relationship with money – all while keeping my integrity and working less hours - so that you can do the same for yourself.

The 10-Minute Memoir

BEST-SELLER

This book came from a deep heartfelt desire to know the stories of my family. Write Your Memoir In Just 10 Minutes A Day With This Easy Q&A Journal

ABOUT ELIZABETH

Elizabeth Menzel is a certified Brennan Healing Science practitioner and serves as a speaker, best selling author, Happy Woman Mentor, and she's the founder of the award winning Happy Woman Academy. Her books and programs focus on ending the cycle of sacrifice, sabotage, and neglect so that women can enjoy massive success in their career, health, and love life.

She uses proven neuroscience and physics based healing systems and has facilitated thousands of transformations over the last 23 years. Her live events & Happiness Training Programs teach busy women of all ages powerful "on the go" ways to heal their body, invigorate their romance, and boost their career – so they can receive more money while enjoying life more fully! She's on a mission to teach 1,000,000 women "The Happy Woman Formula" by 2020.

The mission of the Happy Woman Academy is to provide women with a safe and sacred space to learn how to easily receive more love, health, and money by using proven science based healing systems and the power of communion and laughter.

The vision of the Happy Woman Academy is to restore the Feminine to her rightful place of honor & value next to the Masculine in society, thereby restoring harmonic balance to humanity, the earth, & nature. Big vision I know, but it's the one I've got.

CONNECT WITH ME

Visit www.TheHappyWomanAcademy.com/quiz
And take the 30 second quiz to find out the
#1 way you Sabotage Your Success & Happiness

AND

Visit the Happy Woman Academy on Facebook at
https://www.facebook.com/TheHappyWomanAcademy/

AND

If you'd like 1-1 mentorship with me,
you can apply for a Best Next Step Call @
bit.ly/bestnextstep

AND

I love hearing from my readers, so please feel free to
leave a positive review on my Amazon Author page
at bit.ly/AmazonAuthorElizabethMenzel

CONTENTS

ACKNOWLEDGMENTS

While this book is the culmination of 37 years of personal growth, 10 years of dedicated training, and 22 years of professional practice, I didn't do it alone. I'm deeply grateful to my teachers for putting up with my endless questions, to my clients for ensuring that I hone my skills & keep growing in my capacity to love, and to my dear friends for their care, patience, and riotous laughter. A special thanks to Victor Thompson for cheerfully designing these fabulous book covers and to Stacey & Daniel Canfield at MyImageArtist.com for a magical photo experience.

To Dale Thomas Vaughn, thank you for loving me so completely.

What a special tribe of Vibe Superchargers I have in my life!

Let's all keep Supercharging Our Vibes together!

INTRODUCTION - GET READY

"Fortune and love favor the brave."

— Ovid

Welcome to Supercharge Your Love Vibe! Get ready learn the exact ways I attracted the man of my dreams by changing my broken heart into the well spring of love it's meant to be. As well as how I improved my relationship with my family, my emotions, my body, humanity, and romance, so that you can do the same for yourself. This training course isn't just about romantic love, it helps you supercharge your love vibe in every part of who you are and how you treat yourself and others.

The training exercises in this book are the missing link for many people who have tried everything, yet have hit a wall they can't move past. If you've spent a lot of time, energy, and money trying to improve your relationships and feel more love, then these effective inner world solutions could be the key to the outer world success you have been hoping for.

THIS BOOK IS FOR YOU IF:

You are a good person, but you can't find mister or miss right.

You are trying to get over a broken heart.

Your love life could use more romance.

You are great at many things,

but relationships aren't one of them!

There is a chance you might be too hard on yourself.

You feel stuck and worry that things are never going to change.

You want to feel more compassionate.

You have a ton of love in your life,

AND YOU WANT EVEN MORE!

You've tried everything else, you may as well do all of the exercises in this book and see what happens. But watch out, you might have fun doing them!

A little bit about my love history before we get started on your Love transformation. I was raised in a typical working class family in the Lehigh Valley, in Pennsylvania, but some early childhood Love memories locked in scary beliefs about men, safety, trust, romantic love, platonic love, self worth, and what I thought I deserved. From big things, like my mom and grandmother didn't seem to like their husbands (my father and grandfather) - To bigger things, like my father secretly lived with another woman in another town.

After dad started making a lot of money he abandoned my mom, brother, and I. He lived large with travel, a new Mercedes, a couple of houses, a sailboat, and he even bought a plane, while we dramatically downsized and struggled to get by. By the time I was 13 years old, my mom was working so hard that she stopped regularly cooking, cleaning, or buying groceries. I was pretty much left to support myself, which brought in a whole other wave of denial that buried painful beliefs about love, care, self worth, and not deserving support.

From my early childhood until after my own divorce in my late 30's, my beliefs about relationship were:

- Men leave.
- Men lie.
- Men bully and abuse.
- No one can be trusted.
- I'm a loving person, but I don't get love back.
- I'll never find true love.

I associated romance with feelings of fear, not deserving, and feeling cheated on. I attracted what I knew as love; relationships where the men weren't around much, weren't honest, were bullies, and said one thing but did another. I was often a doormat, with a few outbursts of aggression thrown in here and there to keep things extra painful.

My beliefs on my own self worth were:

- I'm a burden.
- Stay invisible stay safe.
- I don't matter.
- I have to do it all myself, I'm not worth helping.

YIKES! What awful ingredients to try to create a healthy relationship from. My Love Vibe seriously needed an overhaul!

I mostly lived in a state of perpetual heartache, exhaustion, anxiety, and depression. My life was focused on covering basic survival without being able to breakthrough to any better way of living or loving. I thought, "If I just keep trying to fix myself and be the perfect girlfriend, I will win his love." So, I worked extra hard on self-improvement, which is a good thing, except that I was very hard on myself and took all of the blame when others treated me badly.

It didn't occur to me to ask for help with all of the overwhelming things going on in my life. I'd wait for a friend to offer assistance as I couldn't get the words out of my mouth to just ask, "Can you please help me?" Gosh, it hurts to think back to those days.

Thankfully, through years of receiving therapy and healings, I've found and test driven the most effective self healing methods. I use them on myself and teach them to thousands of people worldwide. Contained in this workbook are the exercises I've used to switch from focusing on what is wrong with me to being able to see my strengths and use them for good. Now instead of always feeling nervous - my baseline is one of emotional well-being, happiness, and relaxation. Since 2008 I've shared my life with an honest, loving, funny, sexy, smart, respectful, kind man of integrity that I not only love like crazy, I really LIKE him a lot! I was always good at giving support, but I've learned how to ask for and receive support, and I have incredibly generous friends who have done so much to help me through; I don't think I'd be alive without them!

Since there is always room for improvement, I still practice supercharging my love vibe regularly and I get extra support from my Happy Woman Academy sisters in our monthly WoManifestation Circles™. I actively use the 5 simple steps in my "Happy Woman Formula" every day and I've compiled 50 of the most effective self-healing exercises that are only available in my "Happy Woman Training Program." I understand that you are busy and might not always have tons of extra time, so most everything I teach helps you to retrain your brain and boost your energy while on the go.

Doing everything on your own is just too hard. It's much more fun to go through life supercharging your love vibe with other fun, supportive, awesome women. That's what the Happy Woman Academy is here for! So, NO more going it alone, you are surrounded by allies who want to help you along your healing journey, let us.

No matter what you have been through, you can shed the beliefs that hold you down and move through what holds you back. You can re-wire your brain to create whole new behaviors and experiences. You can learn to love again. I've done it, so I know you can do it too.

CHAPTER 1 - DISCOVER YOUR WHY & FIND YOUR INSPIRATION!

"Loving people live in a loving world.

Hostile people live in a hostile world. Same world."

— Wayne Dyer

Have you ever played with metal tuning forks? If you hold one tuning fork in each hand and hit one of them on something hard the metal vibrates making a sound. Soon the tuning fork that you didn't hit on something hard, that you held perfectly still in your other hand, will start to vibrate and make a sound. This phenomenon is happening all of the time between you and other people and things, and you are so used to feeling it, that you barely even notice it.

But I bet you have experienced it. Have you ever been peacefully sitting there alone reading a book, when suddenly you feel something and can tell someone is standing behind you? Have you ever walked into a room and it just felt good in there? Have you ever been driving the same route home, suddenly decided to make a turn and go a different way, then found out you avoided a huge traffic jam? If you've answered yes to anything even similar to these questions, then you have experienced energetic vibration at work.

And that is because you are made of light, plasma, and sub-atomic particles – in other words, you are made of energy![1]   Energy has a vibration, and that vibration emanates from you - and people and things respond to your vibration, just like the tuning forks. [23] So, when you are feeling great, that vibrational wave is sending out a signal from you and you feel in harmony with anything or anyone around you that is also feeling great. When you are feeling happy, it is easier to notice other happy people around you because you are a vibrational match to them. But when you are feeling lousy, you often notice the other people around you that are feeling lousy. If you are complaining in line at the grocery store, there is soon another person complaining right along with you. But often if you are in a good mood at the check out line, people are really nice and helpful. In little and big ways, everything and everyone around you is constantly responding to your vibration and showing you what you are thinking and feeling by how they treat you and what happens to you.

It's time to stop sending out the vibrations that you don't want; that only works to depress your love vibe, hold you back, and keep you from the love you want.

In order to maintain good relationships you have to choose thoughts, words, and actions of love and connection more often than you choose hatred and separation. See why it's so important for you to supercharge your love vibe and why you were attracted to getting this book? Yes.

Your job is to make yourself the vibrational match to the love that you DO want to have in your life.

But watch out! Shifting into healthy love vibrations can bring up a lot of resistance and fights in your mind, because your mind knows what it is used to feeling as "life" – even if those are feelings you don't like, they are still associated with "Being Alive." So, when you try to change into healthier vibrations, even though they are going to eventually feel better once you get used to them, the mind temporarily registers the new healthy vibration as a threat and equates it to "death." Yes, I'm saying the new healthy love you want can be viewed as so threatening to the old way of life in your mind that you could feel scared enough to not carry forward with trying to feel good. That alone has probably already derailed you from manifesting the love that you want in your life!

As you use the exercises in this workbook that will eventually make you feel like a strong healthy force of LOVE, the resisting thoughts could get louder and might sound something like:

"This is dumb. I don't want to do this any more."

"This isn't going to work, I quit."

"I hate this workbook. Forget it."

"I don't believe this stuff. It probably won't work for me anyway."

The act of resisting feeling good zaps your energy and leaves you feeling depleted and exhausted, which makes it difficult for you to feel love. So even if that level of life vs. death resistance comes up while doing this training course, dig deep and gift yourself this full healing experience. I make it easy for you to get the results you want, but you've got to commit to doing the exercises completely in writing. These exercises may seem simple on the surface, but take a leap of faith and keep moving forward throughout the whole workbook. Go at your own pace, but keep on going. These simple actions create change for the better on a deep level within your mind and brain, and on a practical level in your outer world. I've seen this happen for me and for the thousands of people who I've helped over the last 2 decades.

If you need extra motivation and support, you can easily go to www.TheHappyWomanAcademy.com/quiz and take the "Find out the #1 way you sabotage your success & happiness quiz." This will give you a great jump start plus I'll walk you through a training exercise that you can use to supercharge your love vibe. And there is an additional bonus at the back of this book waiting to reward you AFTER you complete this workbook. Yes, I really want you to heal so much that I'm willing to give you all of this free help!

Here is a weird question, but it could be holding you back so I have to ask you. Is there a chance that you might be afraid of being happy? It took a lot of conscious awareness before I realized that I was often in a state of "bracing myself" waiting for the other shoe to drop. It used to be more obvious, I spent most of the time feeling an underlying constant un-ease until less than a decade ago. A few years ago I noticed that while the unease had greatly reduced, there was this residual sneaky occasional thought, "If I truly feel happy, something bad will come in to wreck it!" Lately I feel happy and grateful much of the time, yet I notice that I'm still holding myself back from feeling truly fantastic all of the time, so there is still room for improvement. This workbook is going to help you if you suffer from feeling nervous about feeling good.

If you happen to judge feeling happy as "not cool," you're going to have a difficult time manifesting the love you want. You might want to consider letting that limiting belief go and replacing it because it's just blocking the love you want to experience from you, and making you less fun at parties. "Feeling happy is cool." See if you can get behind that belief instead.

Even if you've done this course before, doing it again and again can only help you to supercharge your love vibe. You want this for yourself too much to cheat yourself out of this, so I'm going to trust you to follow the instructions and do each and every training exercise. And if you want extra help beyond this training course, I'm here for you. So go for it, keep building those Love muscles! I believe in you, you can do this!

Take a deep breath............ open up your heart and mind.......... and program
yourself to get exactly what you need by stating out loud:

"I fully engage in this training

and get exactly what I need to supercharge my love vibe!"

Make it official:

Signature_____ Date_3/26/22_

SETTING YOU UP FOR SUCCESS

It is easy to buy a workbook and then let it sit on a shelf. I want you to have the transformation that you want and that I know you can have. So, you are going to want to make Supercharging Your Love Vibe your priority over the next few weeks.

1.   Success breeds success. Put time to do these training exercises on your calendar.

Only put an amount of time that seems realistic and easy to achieve. Instead of 1 hour a day, how about 10 minutes a day. Or a 1-hour chunk of time twice a week? Then when you do more than that it's a bonus. But if you do less than that you will feel bad and give up. So, put small doable chunks of time on your calendar and give yourself the enormous gifts this book has in store for you.

2.   Stay accountable, get a buddy.

It's way more fun to do a new activity with someone else that you can relate with. You can keep each other motivated and while it can be easier to break a promise to yourself, it's been proven that you keep your word better if you promise someone else you are going to do something because you don't want to let them down. I give you my full permission to share this workbook with a good ally that you can Supercharge Your Love Vibe with, and have fun keeping each other on track and accountable!

3.   Fully Participate.

For you to get the full benefit of this training course you've got to fully participate. You can't just read through it and understand the concepts and think that will do the trick. Just like you have to do weight training to get stronger muscles, you've got to do all of these exercises to train your love vibe to get stronger. But don't worry, it only takes 1 second to start to supercharge your vibration and after just 17 seconds it picks up momentum to become your new normal! So little by little you will keep getting stronger and supercharging your love vibe.

4.   Write it down

Make sure you write your answers to all of the exercises; don't just answer them in your head. Bring thoughts into the material world by writing them down. You can write your answers directly into this book, or if you got it on Kindle you can just write them out in a notebook or a journal.

The main thing is that you DO EVERY EXERCISE COMPLETELY.

We are going to deeply explore then expand your Love world. So let's jump right in and get started Supercharging your Love Vibe!

Training Exercise 1-1

What is your Why?

I'm sure there are lots of reasons why you want to Supercharge Your Love Vibe. Go ahead and write down the 3 first reasons that come to mind:

1. _to witness the love of my life_
2. _to have better relationship in my life_
3. _to love me + my life._

Great!

Training Exercise 1-2

Now let's get more specific. (If you repeat any of the above reasons, that is ok.) Write down the top reasons why you want to Supercharge Your Love Vibe in each category:

1. Body: _To accept + love my body in all seasons + at all ages._
2. Emotions: _to find compassion for all emotions - to feel my self._
3. Mind: _To improve my outlook w/ more wise - settle my mentally mind_
4. Relationships: _to approach + find growth in the relationships - show up + love better_
5. Career: _To follow my heart + do what I love - share my gift w/ the world_
6. Life Vision: _To be of body with love - like I live it not any closer_
7. Other: _To heal, to transform lives systems. - channel for source - be a mess._

Good. Keep referring to these lists as you go forward through this training. If you regularly practice what I offer here, you will start to witness how this list becomes reality in your day to day life. These lists will keep you inspired to continue your training, so that your Love Vibe grows stronger and stronger.

Training Exercise 1-3

Now, What are the top 3 most valuable things in your life? Write them down quickly without thinking too hard.

1. _My Sobriety_
2. _My Family - bl~_
3. _My purpose._

Good.

Now, look at that last list again.

Are any of those 3 things money?

I didn't think so.

Are any of those 3 things people or have to do with love?

I thought so.

Money is a concept that represents value in society, yet money in and of itself is not A Value. I bring that up right at the beginning because money is so revered in a capitalistic society that people mistakenly replace their personal values with monetary value by judging their worth and importance monetarily. But as you see, the top 3 valuable things in your life aren't all about the Benjamins.

> **Your value as a human is not dependent on money or achievement. I just wanted to take that out of the shadows and bring it into the light.**

Love is the most valuable thing you have to give. Look at how many songs are written about love! Yet, in our society, people mistakenly replace this most precious thing with monetary goals or getting things checked off of their to do list. As if that paperwork, errand, or dirty dishes are more important than kissing your man, hugging your children, or taking care of your health.

> You know love is the most valuable thing you have, so put it in the proper perspective and make LOVE FIRST your motto.

To have a healthy relationship with Love, you can't keep feeding hate with your negative thoughts, words, feelings, and actions.

Brain research shows you have to have 5 times more positive thoughts than negative thoughts just to get to neutral.[4] So let's have 10 more positive thoughts about Love, to make sure you supercharge your Love vibe and starve out all of the negative things you do – probably without even realizing that you are weakening your Love-ability.

To gain a new perspective it can help to depersonalize the concept of love and reframe love simply as an energy. What I noticed is that love is an infinite energy. Money, for example, is a finite energy.

Humans are naturally attracted to infinite energy - it is the energy of life itself, it is the energy you are made of. So, check this out: here you are, this infinite energy based being and you keep trying to force yourself to make finite tasks & money more important than love. That is a huge conflict and to stay unaware of it keeps you suffering with Love problems (and money problems.)

For example, have you ever been guilty of saying anything like the following statements?

- "I promise I'll spend more time with you next month honey, after I get that big account."
- "After I hire a new assistant, clean out all of the closets, and reframe the family photos, then I can go have fun with my girlfriends."
- "I can't go exercise, I haven't gotten enough work done today."

You've got to be willing to ask yourself, "What would love do?" in every situation. Sure, you have responsibilities that are important. But if you are in the habit of neglecting your well being, sacrificing your health, or putting being romantic with your man last on the list – you SERIOUSLY need to Supercharge Your Love Vibe or you'll stay trapped in a downward spiral. Stay on this training course please.

So, how do you create a healthy relationship with love after years of unhealthy beliefs, traumas, and relationships have worn you out?

Admitting the problem is always the first step to healing! Use this training course to help you gain conscious awareness, heal old hurts, and increase your ability to love and be loved in return.

Next up: Where's your Love mind at and what can you do about it?

CHAPTER 2 - REDEFINE YOUR LOVE MIND

"If you would be loved, love, and be loveable."

— Benjamin Franklin

I hope you already got something helpful from Training Exercise 1. Normally I'm giving this workshop to a group of women at a time, and by this point I've already gotten great feedback that shifts are happening! It's all a part of my master plan to make it as easy as possible for women to feel happy, succeed, and thrive!

But remember,

YOU HAVE TO FULLY PARTICIPATE

IN WRITING FOR THIS TO WORK.

Training Exercise 2-1

Without taking a moment to think, fill in the blanks with your knee jerk response.

1.   Dancing is _fun_____.

2.   Clocks are _annoying_____.

3.   The sky is _big_____.

4.   Men are _sexy_____.

5.   Soap is _blah_____.

6.   Mountains are _big_____.

7.   Women are _friendly_____.

8.   Texting is _annoying_____.

9.   Love is _REAL!_____.

Was your last answer a surprise? I'm going to give you more of a chance to expand on that last answer because this is the deal; any positive beliefs you have about Love can attract more Love to you and any negative beliefs you have about Love can block Love from flowing to you. So let's go on a belief busting brainstorm.

Training Exercise 2-2

Set a timer for two minutes and write down every negative belief you can find in your mind about being in love, relationships, men, women, family, intimacy, vulnerability, kindness, love, and gentleness. For example: "love always hurts." Your turn now.

Ready set go!

love never lasts

love hurts

love lets me down

love stress

love comes & goes

I always love to keep going

I'll never find true love

true love doesn't exist

I will never find true love

I'll be alone forever

Love is a fairy tale

No one will ever love me

I am going too old

men cheat

people lie

no one can be trusted

I always attract unavailable men

Exercise 2-3

It's two minutes later now and you've emptied your mind of negative beliefs and since nature abhors a vacuum, you've got to fill your mind with positive beliefs right away. So now you are going to write the opposite of every negative belief from the above list and turn it into a positive statement. For example: "Love always hurts." becomes, "Love always heals." "No one will ever love me because I bruise so easily and my legs look gross." becomes, "My man loves me and accepts me and my legs." (I busted that belief and now have a man that kisses my bruises and loves me as I am and thinks I'm beautiful.) Take all of the time you need to do this.

Ready set go!

Love is forever!

Love heals

Love gives me hope!

Love feels so good!

Love surrounds me all the time!

I chose the right men to love me!

This love has freed me!

I am surrounded by great love!

Love is REAL!

I attract now so much love all the time

Men are trustworthy

People are honest and loving

People are trustworthy

I attract many available men in my life

Training Exercise 2-4

Now, read your positive statements **out loud**. How does it feel when you say those positive statements? Does it feel weird or like a lie? If so, that shows you how strong your negative beliefs are and how hard they were working to block love from easily coming to you and flowing through you.

There is a lot of misinformation out there about positive affirmations. For one, positive affirmations are not simply thinking positively. They work on deeper physical and consciousness levels than just the realm of thoughts. In fact, scientific studies have concluded that your actual DNA can be changed by both positive and negative thoughts, and that unhealthy cells can be made healthy by deep meditation and the frequency change in your brain that positive thoughts stimulate.[56] .[78] In addition to your eye color, you may have also inherited emotional traits through your genes.[9] That's how strong your beliefs are!

Here are my 6 points of clarity about positive affirmations from an energetic perspective:

1.   **If your beliefs aren't working for you they are working against you.** Some of your beliefs are life supporting, some bring you down. The ones that bring you down THINK THEY ARE PROTECTING you, THEY THINK THEY ARE LIFE SUPPORTING beliefs – but they are wrong. When you identify the beliefs that bring you down, it feels weird and scary to try to change them. But if they are not working for you, they are working against you – and that makes life hard and relationships difficult.

2.   **You are always creating from both your conscious and unconscious mind.** That is why it is so important to change those bummer beliefs, so you can consciously create a life you want instead of feeling like a victim of a life you don't like so much. Form follows thought. So you want to make sure that your thoughts are headed in the direction you want your life to go.

3.   **Ultimate health is an open flow of energy**. Control is a tight squeezing energy. So it isn't that positive affirmations give you control, it's that they give the energy of your thoughts a direction. Constantly directing energy towards your vision of a happy, healthy, prosperous, love filled life gives you a better chance of having one.

4.   **Thoughts get stuck in habitual loops** in the brain. A positive affirmation changes course by making a whole new neural pathway![10] This is incredible! As you learned if you ever heard my "Happy Woman Formula" presentation, there is now scientific proof that you can actually re-wire and new wire your physical brain. That takes 30-40 days of consistent new thoughts, talk, and behavior.[11] So let's get you on the path of creating new healthy love habits in your brain today.

5.   **Like attracts like**. The positive affirmation is like a magnet, and it makes your energy field change frequencies from what you don't want to what you do want, and that magnetically attracts like energy to you. If you are radiating at an unhappy frequency, you attract more misery and indifference. Feel like a loser, you lose. Worry about not having enough love, you don't. Radiate at a stronger Love frequency and you attract better relationships and more love.

6.   **Just be willing**. If the positive statement feels just too far fetched, you can back it up a bit until you can feel more of a vibrational match with it. For example, if, "Love always heals" is too much of a stretch for you, try this instead, "I am willing for love to always heal." That opens up your energy flow, and open energy flow is what transformation is all about!

While I provide plenty of scientific studies to back all of this up, the most direct proof is in how you feel after the positive affirmations help get you past the resistance phase. I have been working with this within my own mind and professionally supporting clients in doing the same for decades, and the results in how much better each of us feels is astounding. When I think scary, sad, hopeless thoughts, I feel scared, sad, and hopeless. When I think fun, happy, positive thoughts, I get to feel happy and excited about life. I get more creative and feel energized when I direct my thoughts towards what I do want to experience instead of obsessing about my fears.

You want to feel better? Think better thoughts. It's worked for me and thousands of others. You just have to stick to it for at least a month for it to really start to take hold, get easier, and gain momentum. Then the positive thoughts start to automatically replace the negative thoughts. In the very least, it results in you feeling better. At the best, you create whole new life experiences that are full of satisfaction, enjoyment, and profound love. That alone seems worth sticking with this training!

MAKE YOUR POSITIVE AFFIRMATIONS AS POWERFUL AS POSSIBLE:

• Always keep them in present tense.

• Have fun with them.

• Always say them out loud.

• Repeat them often, hundreds of times a day if you can.

• Make sure when you say them you get some kind of physical sensation in your body.

• Make sure when you say them you get an increase in emotional feelings.

(Those last 2 are how you know they are working.)

So far you've gotten clear on Why you want to supercharge your love vibe, you've emptied out your negative love beliefs and replaced them with positive ones, you've gotten the lowdown on why positive affirmations are so powerful, and you know how you can use them every day to become a love magnet and increase your love ability.

Repeat your positive statements out loud every day and let this sink in and start making new love-filled neural pathways in your brain as you also supercharge your love vibration in your energy system. Then you'll be ready to go to the next level in Supercharging Your Love Vibe!

"We are what we repeatedly do;

excellence then is not an act,

but a habit."

Aristotle

Next up: Neediness & Worthiness.

CHAPTER 3 - NEEDY BY NATURE, WORTHY BY EXISTENCE

"I have decided to stick with love. Hate is too great a burden to bear."
— Martin Luther King, Jr.

This next topic comes up a lot with my clients and it was something that I had to heal to supercharge my love vibe. Let me ask you this: If all humans are indeed created equal, is it true that you could be "less than" any other human on the planet?

No. No possible way.

Yet so many people have issues around self worth and deserving that they end up placing themselves below another human. And that gets tied in with shame about neediness and feeling guilty for having any kind of need… at all… ever.

I could go on and on about self worth and neediness, it's long and convoluted and full of psychological gymnastics. But I'm here to help you heal, so I like to keep the healing effective and results oriented, so I come back to two basic facts:

1.   We are all created equal, so you can't be better or worse or deserve more or less than anyone else.

2.   You are human, therefore, you have needs.

You have basic survival needs: air, food, water, shelter. Then you have basic thrive needs such as: respect, understanding, trust, love. (For a complete list of Basic Human Needs please refer to Rosenberg, Marshal B. (2003) "Non-Violent Communication: A Language of Life" and Maslow, A.H. (1943). "A theory of human motivation." *Psychological Review* 50 (4) 370–96.)

When you were born, you needed constant care from others or you would have died. You were totally dependent. As you grew, you gradually learned to take care of your own needs and become more independent. As you matured, you learned when it's best to take care of yourself and when it's best to ask for help. Well, in a perfect world you learned when it's best to take care of yourself and when it's best to ask for help, but you may really struggle with asking for help or taking care of yourself first.

Can you relate to this? You vacillate between feeling helpless and co-dependent, thinking lowly of yourself, and devaluing your skills - to taking every burden onto your shoulders and striking out alone, doing it all yourself and not accepting/asking for help. I've noticed after more than two decades of helping people heal that a lot of suffering occurs by vacillating between these two painful places.

The truth remains, you are human therefore you have needs, so you've got to accept the fact that you are needy by nature and worthy by existence and let that set you free.

When you fight against your healthy, natural human needs you create an energy block in your system that keeps you from receiving the love, money, and health you want. You deny the basic natural order that all beings are created equal when you put yourself down, hold yourself back, and think negative thoughts about yourself and others.

Whenever you take on too much by yourself without receiving help when you really could use it, you tell the Universe that you DON'T want the gifts it has for you. The Universe sent you a person or thing to help you out, and you told the Universe "NO." So then the Universe gets the message, "Oh, she can't receive so she obviously doesn't want to be given nice things. Ok, got it. Don't give her nice things."

Conversely, when you don't stand strongly on your own two feet and strike out on your own sometimes, you deny the magnificently resilient energy you are made of the chance to prove to you your inner strength.

It might seem tricky, but you can learn how to be strong on your own – AND - strong asking for help. Strong alone – AND – in relationship. Your words, thoughts, feeling, and actions are training the Universe – and other people - how to treat you.

> **If you want to receive more money, love, and good health, you must allow yourself to be honest about your true worth and your true needs as they truly are in each moment.**
> **That's a lot of truthiness.**

Sometimes what blocks your ability to supercharge your love vibe is feelings of guilt from someone you've wronged in the past, so you feel like you don't deserve love. You may have hurt yourself or someone else so deeply that you can't forgive yourself.

Here is my recipe for forgiveness:

1) Apologize to the person/people you hurt. Take responsibility WITHOUT EXCUSES for the painful action and sincerely say, "I'm sorry I did _____. I feel true remorse, I know it was painful, and I sincerely apologize. I am truly sorry."

2) Ask what you can do to make amends, then actually follow through and do it. Even if you can't actually make up for it, you can still take action to help the healing process. Yes, you can even do this for yourself when you've hurt yourself!

3) Become trustworthy by taking whatever healthy action you can to improve your behavior and promise YOURSELF that you will not do the harmful action again.

4) If you knew better you would do better, and now you know better. But at the time you did the harmful thing, you might have been doing the best you could for the awareness you had. Accept that you are human and make mistakes, and be willing to forgive yourself. Forgiveness can be hard to do and you can't force true forgiveness. So, just be willing to forgive yourself.

5) The other person may or may not be able to forgive you and that is their right. Apologize, take responsibility for your part, make amends through positive action, be willing to forgive yourself, and let the other person have their feelings about you, no matter what they are. Give them the freedom they deserve because...

"Would you rather be right or free?"
~ Byron Katie

I choose love and freedom. I hope you can to.

The thing that is going to heal you is love. Give yourself permission to supercharge your love vibe and allow more and more love to flow through you, so you can improve your behavior and your circumstances and start the forgiveness process.

If you have deep issues around self worth, guilt, needs, and deserving, don't worry, you really can heal these issues and come to a whole new way of being and feeling in your life. Keep moving forward through this training course, and if you'd like more help on your healing journey, I'm here for you.

Training Exercise 3-1

Remember, at your core you are not better or worse than anyone else, and they are not better or worse than you. You are equal and no more or less deserving of love.

Without comparing yourself to anyone else, write down 3 skills you have that you enjoy.

1. _I am a great coat-engage others_ – _tb my husband_ –
   I feel great- I an in love
2. _I am inspiring & motivating_ – _I an helpi's_   _whe –it serves_
   own – it makes me to other
3. _I work really well._   _feel good to help other_
   by grs others it means not

Next to each skill write how that benefits your life.   _enesiri sid._

For example:

a)   Skill I enjoy: Making costumes.

Benefit to self: Fun, move creative energy, joy, problem solving, communion with Dale (my man.)

b)   Skill I enjoy: Seeing both sides of an argument.

Benefit to self: Feel love and equanimity, exercise my brain, grow my capacity to love and accept, communion with fellow humans.

c)   Skill I enjoy: Hiking.

Benefit to self: Ground, improve coordination & fitness, connect with nature, see new things from a new perspective.

Now it's your turn:

1.   Skill I enjoy: _I am a good coach. coaching/helping others_
How I benefit: _love who, connection, LOVE, since Steven my_
par helps me
2.   Skill I enjoy: _Motivating, inspiring_
How I benefit: _them me say it out loud feels in._
I questioned - trusted work,
3.   Skill I enjoy: _Writing_
How I benefit: _Creative, perspective. Fun, helps others_
learn

Great, write all of that down for real. This course will not supercharge your love vibe if you do it all in your head. You MUST bring it into the physical realm by writing it down.

Now next to your above answers, fill in how that might benefit others.

For example:

1.   Making costumes.

Benefit to self: Fun, move creative energy, joy, problem solving, communion with Dale

Benefit to others: people laugh, feel inspired, and lighten up. Move creative energy on the planet.

2.   Seeing both sides of an argument.

Benefit to self: Feel love and equanimity, exercise my brain, grow my capacity to love and accept, communion with fellow humans.

Benefit to others: Increase love and respect between humans on the planet, decrease war promote peace.

3.   Hiking.

Benefit to self: Grounding, Improve coordination & fitness, connect with nature.

Benefit to others: I often help people with directions when I hike, inspire others to get fit, I clean up trails, I give money to the Sierra club and to support national and state parks that protect land, I give money to manufacturers of quality gear, I increase respect for mother earth and keep healthy energy moving on the planet, I take women hiking with me the first Saturday of every month.

1. Skill I enjoy:_____*[handwritten]*_____

    How I benefit:_____

    How another benefits:___*[handwritten]*___

2. Skill I enjoy:___*[handwritten]*___

    How I benefit:_____

    How another benefits:___*[handwritten]*___

3. Skill I enjoy:___*[handwritten]*___

    How I benefit:_____

    How another benefits:___*[handwritten]*___
    [handwritten]

See?

Just doing the things you enjoy doing

can be a benefit to others!

Now sit back and bask in the glow

of what a valuable asset you are in the world!

Training Exercise 3-2

Do you ever find yourself saying really mean things inside your own head? Well guess what? Self-deprecating talk won't get you more love. That mean trash talk will only hold you back as your loveless words deny the power that is the wondrous energy that made you. Honoring the truth of your very Being is what opens up the love super highway because it supercharges the energy frequency you're putting out to the world, which affects what you get back from the world.

So start shifting this right here right now.

Stand up.

Get up off of your butt.

Say out loud:

> "I am worthy of love. I am worthy of peace.
> I am worthy of healthy relationships. I allow all of the love
> I want to easily come to me and I receive it."

Niiiice. Try saying this before every meal for the next week. No, I'm not kidding. Write it down on several post-its. Place it in the center of your steering wheel, on your mirror, in your pocket, & in your wallet! Repeat it as often as you possible, hundreds of times a day! You want to make a strong neural pathway of self worth so that you can supercharge your love vibe.

Training Exercise 3-3:
Go from mean trash talk – to Luscious Love Lips for the next 24 hours!

There is an old saying I learned from Florence Scovel Shinn that reminds us of the power of our words: "YOUR WORD IS YOUR WAND." Every time you hear yourself say, or about to say something like, "I'm so scared I'll always be alone." Use your word as your wand to state what you DO want instead. "I'm so happy that I'm surrounded by people who love me!" "I'm so relieved that the drivers in Trader Joe's parking lot are kind to me." – you can say that on your way to the grocery store. Imprint what you do what to happen onto your subconscious mind. Have fun with it. Some of my favorite mantras, "I love myself through every situation." "I find something to love about my incredible man every day!" "I love and accept myself as I am." Now that's luscious love lips!

Try this for 24 hours, no mean trash talk, only words of love – then see how you feel. I guarantee that will supercharge your love vibe and you will want to keep it up! The more you do it, the stronger you feel and the easier it gets!

Next up: Make your peace with the natural energy flow of the Universe.

CHAPTER 4 - THE NATURAL FLOW OF THE UNIVERSE: GIVING AND RECEIVING

"The giving of love is an education in itself."
— Eleanor Roosevelt

Now that you own that you are a worthy person, you accept that you are a human therefore you have needs, you started forgiving yourself, you reprogrammed your system to allow love to move through you, and you have ended the mean trash talk and replaced it with words of love, let's get you in harmony with the most natural cycle in life: Giving and Receiving.

A carrot plant receives sunshine, rain, and nutrients from the soil so it can grow, it then gives us nutrients for our health, we exhale and the carrot plant receives our carbon dioxide giving us back oxygen.

Giving and receiving is how life on earth is sustained.

It is common to go numb to all of the love being given to you when you aren't open to receiving it. If you've been traumatized, verbally or physically abused, or just were somehow given confusing messages about safety, care, or nurturance, it's really hard to simply receive because what came to you in the past wasn't always safe, wanted, or right for your wellbeing.

The problem now is that by trying to protect yourself from harmful things, you also block the flow of good things coming to you! Giving and receiving are a two way street on one road that needs to keep clear so the flow can go back and forth in a natural harmonious way.

Training Exercise 4-1

You can't change the past, but you can decide

to open yourself to the goodness

that the Universe has for you today

by affirming out loud,

"I am open to the love the Universe has for me

and I safely receive love now."

Go ahead and shout that one out loud.

Good.

Training Exercise 4-2

When you think about something, your brain thinks it is actually happening.[1213] So, give yourself permission anywhere, anytime, to think about the things and people you love and that will boost your love vibe!

Something I enjoy doing to boost my love vibe is to tap into nature; I just went up on my roof to bask in the full moon. I can sit here in my chair and recall the feeling of hiking up a mountain, the dust and dirt swirling around me, the smell of the trees and soil, the sound of the wind. I remember sitting next to the Colorado River, how it smelled and the music of the water. Oh I just love the earth so much! I love thinking about my man, how his green eyes gaze into mine, looking straight through me. I remember nice things friends have done for me last week – as well as 10, 20, 30 years ago! I think of my mom's piercing laugh and how her eyes get sparkly when she's laughing hard. All of these things connect me to the abundant love that exists all around me. They instantly remind me that the Universe is full of love and is always giving and receiving love through me.

Next, let's clear up a common misconception around giving and receiving. People often have negative ideas that giving means giving it all away, overdoing it from obligation, or giving yourself up. They also have negative ideas that receiving means taking or being selfish, and those negative ideas make guilt and shame grow. Those concepts are the dark side of giving and receiving that get expressed when they are out of balance, but there is a light side too! When you are in touch with your loving heart and living in balance, you give and receive equally, happily, and cleanly. This is the way that both giving and receiving feel awesome.

If you try to separate giving from receiving you'll feel exhausted, overwhelmed, burned-out, resentful, get sick easily, and your love problems will persist. It's necessary to receive rest, love, healthy food, money & joy, so that you can give it back to others.

I've made it my life's mission to help women keep their successful *career without sacrificing their health or relationships. *I include motherhood as a full time job and admirable career choice. If you rob energy from your health, children, or marriage in order to keep your career going – you will crash and burn and end up sabotaging all you hold dear. Every aspect of your life will suffer if you don't put your well-being at the top of your list. You can't give from a dry well forever and all of that giving from obligation makes you resentful as well as depleted and exhausted. I've seen it too many times in my clients and I witnessed it in my mother and grandmother who neglected their own well-being and marriages, in the name of work and the glorification of busy. Tending to your inner world is serious business. I'm so glad you are committed to seeing this training course all of the way through so that you can give and receive in just the right amount to keep you healthy, wealthy, and in love with your life.

So let's continue to unstick the places you might be stuck; and to open up the giving and receiving flow of energy inside of you, bringing your inner and outer world into harmony and supercharging your love vibe. You may feel very resistant to actually do the following exercises. That resistance proves how much you need to do it, so get to it!

Training Exercise 4-3

Stand up. Get out of your chair and move. Shake your body, shake it out.

Plant your feet shoulder width apart, bend your knees, place both hands on the center of your breast bone over your heart energy center. Now think of one of your closest friends. Think of how much goodness you want this person to have. Doesn't it feel great to love them and wish them good things?

See your friend in your mind's eye and imagine giving your friend a big blast of your love! Shine out your love to them. See them happy and smiling and healthy.

Imagine them safe and having what they want and need to feel good. Remember a time when you laughed so hard together that you had no thoughts, just pure joy coursing through you. Send your dear friend another big blast of love from your heart.

Yes, that feels so great to give your love and positive thoughts to this wonderful loving person. Take some moments and do not move on to the next section until you stand up, plant your feet should width apart, and actually do this exercise right now.

Aaaah… that feels amazing!

Take a deep cleansing breath.

Training Exercise 4-4

Now let yourself remember the kind things this person has done for you. Think about the times they had your back, cheered you up, celebrated with you, and supported you.

> Take a deep breath into your heart, fling your arms wide open,
>
> and shout out loud,
>
> **"THANK YOU FOR LOVING ME!"**

You've got to let yourself actually physically and verbally do this (or you can just keep blocking the love you say you want). You can do it! Prove to the Universe you are ready to receive. Really feel the gratitude you have for your friend's love and care. Let their love in. Soak up their love like a giant sea sponge. Allow their wonderful giving to shower you and sink into you. (This exercise always makes me tear up. I just did it again, my eyes are leaking.)

It feels so great when I give to someone and they sincerely appreciate it. But, giving doesn't feel as good when it is not happily received by the other person. I want to see the people I love happy. I know you want to let yourself receive because you are taking this training course. You will automatically supercharge your love vibe as you supercharge your ability to receive. So, allow yourself to truly receive when people do nice things for you, then your receiving becomes the gift you give back to them.

That is how it works here on earth. Do you want to receive love? You have to make sure you are OPEN and that your giving comes from your loving heart and that you let yourself receive with joy and gratitude.

Try doing these two Training Exercises with at least 2 more people in mind. Get very specific about seeing your loved ones in your mind's eye and giving then receive a big love blast to and from them.

I understand that it can seem scary or hard to receive, that is why I want you to practice by thinking of people that you trust and love, so that your energy system can learn what it feels like to safely receive, heal, and get better and better at receiving. As you practice doing it in the safety and privacy of your own space alone, you'll build strength to be able to do it with people and things outside of your little world.

There is a huge difference in your vibration when you allow yourself to have what you want, if only in your thoughts and feelings, because it conditions you to allow yourself to get what you want. Get it? Keep going, you are doing great!

Next up: A way to practice gratitude that really works to supercharge your love vibe.

CHAPTER 5 - SHOW GRATITUDE IN WHAT YOU THINK, SAY, AND DO!

"The more one judges, the less one loves."

— Honore de Balzac

It's important to practice strengthening the energy frequency of gratitude in regards to love because gratitude tells the Universe, "Yes please. Give me more of this good stuff I like. Thank you!" I mean hey, when someone sincerely says, "Thank you" to you, doesn't it automatically make you want to give them more? Yes! See, the Universe works just like you do!

Have you ever had your water or electricity in your house turned off? You can't bathe or do the dishes. The food in the refrigerator can go bad, you can't turn on the heat, you can't get work done on your computer, your phone dies and you miss an important work call and can't get in touch with your family – it can really throw you off.

BUT YET...

Have you ever rushed through your day and NOT once thought THANK YOU when water comes out of the tap or the lights turn on?

Of course - everyone has done that! I actually started this gratitude practice when I was 16 years old and living on my own. I had never heard of doing this before, I didn't know anything about conscious manifestation or the power of gratitude. I was just a teenage girl all alone, fending for myself, in this beautiful apartment that I worked really hard to keep. And I was so sincerely grateful that I had lights, a refrigerator, and a roof over my head, that I'd write out each check for my bills and think, "Thank God I can cover the gas bill!" This practice gives you so much more of a feeling of power and unleashes the abundance of love you have in your heart. How about feeling gratitude instead of feeling angry every time you pay a bill?

I'm inviting you to give gratitude for the basics so that you can build a foundation of thankfulness, strengthen your gratitude muscle, and supercharge your love vibe even more.

Let's start by thinking more thankfully.

Training Exercise 5-1

Write down 5 things you are very grateful to have in your every day life.
For example: I'm so grateful that when I turn on the tap clean water comes out!
I'm so thankful I have enough money to pay the electric bill and keep the lights on!

1. _I am so grateful I have a roof over my head_
2. _I am so grateful I have good food in the fridge_
3. _I am so grateful to have hot & clean water_
4. _I am so grateful to can cover all my bills_
5. _I am so grateful I can take care of my daily needs._ ♡

Write down 5 thoughts you could think that would show more gratitude and appreciation towards your self and your body.

For example: I'm so grateful that my heart keeps beating!

I'm so thankful that I could make it to the gym today.

I did a great job of not yelling at the kids when they put clay in the fountain.

1. _[handwritten]_
2. _[handwritten]_
3. _[handwritten]_
4. _[handwritten]_
5. _[handwritten]_

Sometimes it is easier to show gratitude to people you don't know as well, like the barista, while others that are closer to you tend to get overlooked. You've got to give appreciation to yourself and others in order to get it.

Write down 5 people that you could say thank you to more often. Then say "thank you" and explain how they improve your life the next time you talk to them.

For example: "Thank you Dale for being so loyal and trustworthy. It allows me to feel safe with you and relax into your arms more securely."

1. _[handwritten]_
2. _[handwritten]_
3. _[handwritten]_
4. _[handwritten]_
5. _[handwritten]_

Whether or not you have a partner, write down at least 5 actions you can take that express love and gratitude to your partner (real or imagined) in a way that you know they will like.

For example: Give a massage to Dale.

1. _Cook beautiful healthy meals for him_
2. _give him a long back or foot massage_
3. _Ask just this anything to do._
4. _help him with a task that has been bothering him_
5. _take an evening all about him - Shower him_
   with sexy attention

Then take action and do at least one loving thing that shows your gratitude every day until you die. Keep coming up with new ways to show your love and appreciation for your awesome partner! Romantic love is like a campfire. You don't just light it once and expect it to keep burning. You have to tend to the fire every few minutes, putting in new kindling, nudging logs around, throwing a new log on the fire. That is the only way the fire keeps burning and that is the only way your romance stays alive! My man compliments me and finds new ways to say and show love EVER DAY. I've really had to supercharge my love vibe to meet his high vibration! Neither one of us is perfect, but we tend to our romantic fire many times a day. And instead of that being tiring, it energizes our relationship and 7.5 years in it still feels fresh and exciting.

What if you think your partner is not awesome? That is going to require extra care and help to sort through and see what is really going on. Keep practicing supercharging your love vibe and also get professional help; either from me or another mentor, healer, or therapist, to gain the clarity you need about your relationship.

Training Exercise 5-2

Take a deep breath, place both hands over your heart center in the middle of your breast bone, and sincerely thank each of these things and people listed above for the goodness they bring into your life.

An attitude of gratitude and saying THANK YOU when people & things add goodness to your life strengthens your Love ability and supercharges your Love Vibe.

Training Exercise 5-3

Think back to a time when something happened that you did NOT want to happen, yet, somehow something EVEN BETTER happened because of it and you ended up feeling so grateful that it happened that way. Write about what you learned from that experience, and the GOOD that came from it.

This is a VERY important training exercise, no skipping over it.

I was so sad after [illegible] and I broke up - devastated. Heaven, that got me going to rowing & Hawaii & I did. That move to Hawaii was the best move of my life. I met great people and I got sober!

~~[illegible]~~

My sobriety has given me everything - new friends, love for god, reconnection of Self! - Better relationships, passion & courage to pursue goals, my love.

THE UNIVERSE IS FOR ME!

See, sometimes you think things are going wrong, when actually they are going right! This training exercise proves how important it is to be as thankful as possible in your thoughts, words, and actions every day, no matter what is happening in your life.

As a freelance entrepreneur, I've had to learn to roll with last minute changes, and trust that everything will work out – and so far it has for over 2 decades! Whenever a client changes their appointment, instead of freaking out I say, "Oh, I guess the Universe is giving me the afternoon off. Now I can write/ hike/ get a massage." Often, one client changes their appointment minutes before another client calls for an emergency session at that same time – and magically I have the space for them!

Accepting life's sudden changes is a huge trust builder, and trusting makes you feel better than worrying, and feeling better makes you vibrate at a higher love frequency, and that higher love frequency makes you feel more love, and that is the opposite of stress so you get to relax and enjoy your life MORE, and that attracts more loving people and situations to you, and you get to keep supercharging your love vibe despite what life throws at you. Some days are easier than others, but you can do this!

There is an old saying, "Your ship comes in over calm waters." So, when you can feel thankful and trust that you are going to be ok and take positive action to care for your health, creativity, and well being, you trigger positive momentum. That positive momentum feels great and clears a path for more positivity to come to you.

At the very least, freaking out feels bad, giving gratitude for what is as it is and trusting it to get even better feels good. Which way would you rather feel? Which vibration do you think is more likely to attract the love you want?

Remember, you work how the Universe works – the Universe works how you work. You love being thanked and it makes you want to give more. The Universe loves being thanked and it makes it want to give you more. Test drive this law of universal energy flow. I've been using it for years to feel more love and I am living proof that the exercises in this book work!

Training Exercise 5-4

Is there someone in your life that does a lot for you – or just seems to be doing a lot for people in general? Maybe you have some making up to do and a special favor for someone would be a great way to show your real gratitude for their kindness and efforts. Take action and show some extra appreciation for this special person by doing something very kind that you know they'd like. Put it in your calendar so you are sure it gets done.

Perhaps there is a person or organization that really inspires you. You could volunteer or tithe some money to them to express your gratitude and give them a boost of motivation. Everyone loves feeling appreciated, pass that feeling on and see how great it feels!

It's easy to blame the world for working against you instead of paying attention to all of the little ways things are working for you every day. These exercises wake you up so you can notice the goodness that is already there. What you look at is what you see and what you focus on grows. Gratitude helps you notice that more love is present than you realized. You'll even start to feel grateful when things don't go your way, because that is a sign that 1) you need to supercharge your love vibe and 2) perhaps you're being set up for something even better!

Infusing your thoughts, words, feelings and actions with an extra dose of gratitude gives you the power to create your own healthy vibrant loving world!

Next up: Why wait to feel the love you want?

CHAPTER 6 - DON'T WAIT, FEEL LOVE NOW!

"Love is not only something you feel, it is something you do."
— David Wilkerson

So, you know why you want to supercharge your love vibe, but don't you also wonder what it would FEEL like to have so much love that you feel it all of the time – even when you are sleepy, angry, or confused? Sure that might sound contradictory, but love exists beyond emotions, so it is there no matter what emotion you are feeling. You don't have to wait for all of your old problems to be resolved or for you to be with the perfect partner - you get to practice feeling love all of the time right now. You can start small by doing little things that make you feel love without waiting for outside circumstances to change.

Training Exercise 6-1

Write down 3 ways that you already experience love in your life.

1. _Blue's looks of me - Letch her slap_
2. _thinking about love_
3. _Seeing cute baby or puppy - the energy that loves is in me_

Training Exercise 6-2

There is a happy loving person inside of you just waiting to be unleashed! Take 3 super slow and deep breaths while you allow the love you already have inside of you to come alive and on the fourth breath say out loud,

"I activate the love within me. I feel in love now!"

Over the next few weeks, keep noticing ways that you already feel love and really let yourself enjoy feeling it each time. This strengthens your love awareness and supercharges your love vibe.

Here it is, the exercise you've been waiting for! The one everyone begs me to teach them! This is how I went from years of tragic relationships and inner hurt, to supercharging my love vibe so thoroughly that I attracted the love of my life. Use this method to attract the types of friendships and romance that you do want in your life, and to transform the relationships you are in. I'll give you an extra special bonus proof at the end of this exercise so you can see how this worked for me again a couple of months ago, just in a slightly different way.

Training Exercise 6-3

Tonight, after you get into bed, think about the type of relationship you want to be in. Imagine yourself in very specific scenarios with this person. What does it look like around you? What is the temperature? Are you at home? Traveling? Walking down the street? Having dinner together? You can choose a different scene every time if you want. Get creative and let your imagination run wild.

What does it FEEL like to be with this person? How does he hold you? What are the sensations in your body just being next to him? Are you relaxed and excited?

Does he make you laugh? Whatever it is you WANT to feel with your beloved, that is how you allow yourself to feel, right now, as you lay there falling asleep.

Sweet dreams.

I did this every single night for 2 years. I fell asleep actually feeling like I was right there with my dream man. I often envisioned us on a colorfully tiled balcony overlooking the Mediterranean Sea. I don't know why I kept seeing this scene, but there it was. I could feel the breeze, smell the sea, feel his arms around me, hear us quietly talking, laughing, and feel us kissing. Isn't that a better way to fall asleep than feeling alone and frustrated?

When you wake up in the morning, allow yourself to have those same love feelings & imaginings RIGHT AWAY. Don't hesitate or else lonely consciousness can set in quickly and make you feel as if you aren't made of love. You are doing this to supercharge your love vibe, so supercharge it first thing in the morning and think about it often to keep it going all day!

When this was my daily practice, every single morning I awoke and wouldn't let myself get out of bed until I felt my man there with me and I had an authentic smile on my face! Sometimes this would take a couple of minutes, but sometimes I had so much resistance to feeling love and happiness that it would take an hour! But, I was totally committed to supercharging my love vibe and I never started my day without feeling in love with this awesome man. After the first 6 months of doing this night and day, the questions started coming in from friends and colleagues, "Have you met someone?" "You are glowing. Are you in love?" I got asked so many times if I was in love and I always answered the same way, "I AM in love, I just haven't met him yet!"

This is the secret, I felt totally in love all day long! I had a tickle in my belly and I'd giggle for no reason. My years of worry, loneliness, and tragic relationships were

OVER. I no longer pined, I no longer lamented, I was in LOVE! I had no man in the physical world YET, but I sure felt like I had him in every other way! And I knew, **I knew** he would find me because my love vibe, my beacon to the right partner for me, was getting stronger and more specific every single day.

One of the reasons you want a healthy relationship is to feel happy and loved. So don't deny that everything isn't already inside of you. Keep practicing and let yourself feel love, and anything else you want to feel, NOW.

Like sonar waves emanating out from you, your vibration both attracts and repels. Consciously creating what you DO want to experience is always about imagining it, saying it, feeling it, and letting your actions and the actions of the Universe respond to your vibrations. So you want to be sending out the right vibes that attract what you want to happen in your life. New thoughts appear, new circumstances arise, and new actions get taken when you shift your thoughts and your energy from lack to the true abundance of the energy you are made of.

The feeling of Love is a part of what you want the good relationships for anyway, so you don't need to wait for outside changes to determine your inner feelings. Give yourself the feeling now and cut a clear pathway that allows love to easily come through you from the inside and to you from the outside, then you can Feel and BE love in this moment. Not some potential future date, but right NOW. Feel everything you want right now.

> ## "I Am Loving and Thriving NOW."
> ## "I am Happy, healthy, and in love Now."

My most recent favorite mantra that has been working really well for me is this: every morning I affirm, "I get everything I NEED to get done, DONE today." That feels so much better than worrying that I am falling behind. If by the end of the day everything on my to-do list didn't get done, it must not have actually needed to! This way I am always staying on the Universe's course, instead of my ego's course. Instead of creating a war inside me by putting myself down, I'm much more grateful for all I accomplished, and loving & accepting about the tasks I did not complete.

I can be very slow at doing things, so to affirm, "I have the perfect pace" really calms me down and helps me feel centered and strong. If you keep thinking and talking about the gap from where you are to where you want to be – guess what happens? That gap widens!! You have the power to eradicate that gap. Feel what you want to feel NOW, don't wait for some imaginary future.

I said I'd give you some bonus proof for how this works so well. For our entire relationship, my man and I have been very happy with each other – except in one area. We have had many deep talks and have tried so many things, but nothing seemed to make the change we wanted in this one particular situation. So, I decided to use this same method to help me change my vision of him from one of struggle to one of success. I started envisioning him happy in this area of his life.

When I started to feel myself getting frustrated with him I would say, "I trust this will change. Until then, I will love him, he loves me, and we will get through this."

And I just kept envisioning and feeling this particular situation being different than it was – and he has been envisioning it and feeling it as well and he applied the training techniques from one of my other books!

It has only been 2 months, yet so many new opportunities have been attracted to him since he started supercharging his vibration in this area that it is blowing us away!

There is still progress to be made, but we have never felt more optimistic or positive that the change we seek on the outside is coming soon, because we are really practicing feeling it on the inside!

Our 8 year anniversary is coming up in May and I'm still in love with this wonderful man... and I have been for 10 years (even though I only met him 7.5 years ago!)

So far you've already shifted some painful love beliefs that were holding you back, supercharged your inner love vibration, opened the flow of giving and receiving, gotten clear on why you want more love, reprogrammed your system to allow love to move through you, claimed the power of speaking words of love, given love to your body, made peace with neediness and self worth, started forgiving yourself, shifted to an attitude of gratitude, and started to vibrate at the energetic frequency of love now.... But are you in alignment?

Find out in the next chapter, lucky #7, Get Into Centered Alignment

CHAPTER 7 - GET INTO CENTERED ALIGNMENT

"Love many things, for therein lies the true strength, and whosoever loves much performs much, and can accomplish much, and what is done in love is done well."

— Vincent Van Gogh

If you've been putting into practice all that you've learned along this course, you've probably already seen some shifts in your love world and how you feel about love. By this point many people have told me little and big things that have changed for them, which is very exciting. These inner secrets are what so many people miss out on when trying to improve their love life. Be sure to read and practice all the way to the end of this book so you can stay on course supercharging your love vibe like a boss!

Have you ever noticed that sometimes you are just totally in the zone and everything comes easily to you and you just get stuff done? Then there are times where doing even things you normally enjoy is like trying to push a boulder up a hill? When I'm struggling against the current, feeling miserable, and putting tons of effort into something but not enjoying it at all because there is no flow, I know what is wrong. I'm out of centered alignment. Centered alignment with what? With my highest good in that moment. Allow me to explain.

You may have so many responsibilities and things you "have to get done" that your life is run by all of those obligations and outside forces determining your every move. When you live that way, life feels like a grind. Even simple things like folding laundry or driving to work are a struggle. But when your actions are preceded by aligning with your highest good and bringing yourself to your centered inner power, even doing the dishes can feel joyful, and your meaningful work/ art/ studying/ parenting, FEELS FANTASTIC TO DO!

When you are in centered alignment with your highest good:

- **Creativity is boosted and new ideas keep popping up**
- **You roll up your sleeves and joyfully take care of business**
- **Challenges get tackled and feel satisfying**
- **You enjoy taking care of your body and make sure you get enough exercise, nourishing food, and rest.**
- **When sudden changes occur you go with the flow and don't let it throw you off.**
- **You get paid your worth and money flows to you more easily.**
- **You feel happy about today and excited about your future.**
- **You feel in love - not just with your partner, but with life.**

Do you want to feel that way every day? I do! I teach an immersive program on how to bring yourself into centered alignment with your highest good called the "The Happy Woman Formula." Be sure to enter TheHappyWomanAcademy.com so you can get in on that action – you'll get a free exercise as a thank you gift. Bonus!

You've made it to the final exercise of the Supercharge Your Love Vibe Training - congratulations!

Training Exercise 7-1

Sit comfortably and take a deep breath into your belly… and let it out. Let the next inhale come all of the way into your hips… and exhale. Relax your shoulders. Give yourself some quiet time to center in first.

Then when you are relaxed and centered, read the below questions and allow your deepest wisdom to answer frankly and honestly. DO NOT EDIT OR THINK – just let your inner voice be heard, take pen to paper, and circle your answer. You may be surprised at what happens.

Circle where you are at on this scale of 1-10.
(1 is No not at all and 10 is 100% Yes)

1.   Do you give your body everything it needs to be nourished and fit?
     1   2   3   4   5   6   7   8   (9)   10

2.   Do you get enough rest?
     1   2   3   4   (5)   6   7   8   9   10

3.   Do you get enough social time with friends?
     1   2   (3)   4   5   6   7   8   9   10

4.   Are your thoughts about yourself encouraging and kind?
     1   2   3   4   (5)   6   7   8   9   10

5.   Do your words reflect the real love you feel for those closest to you?
     1   2   3   (4)   5   6   7   8   9   10

6.   Are the friends you see the most often accepting of who you are and only want what is best for you?
     1   2   3   4   5   6   (7)   8   9   10

7.   Is the romantic relationship you are currently in supportive and happy for both of you?

    1   2   3   4   5   6   7   8   9   10

8.   Is there enough romance in your love-life?

    (1)   2   3   4   5   6   7   8   9   10

9.   Do you feel valued and fairly compensated in your job?

    1   2   3   4   5   6   (7)   8   9   10

10. Are you willing to make amends with people you have wronged, including yourself?

    1   2   3   4   5   6   7   8   9   (10)

11. Are you willing to forgive yourself?

    1   2   3   4   5   6   7   8   9   (10)

12. Are you willing to let yourself feel love many times a day?

    1   2   3   4   5   6   7   8   9   (10)

13. Is your home a safe haven?

    1   2   3   4   5   6   7   8   9   (10)

14. Does your work feel satisfying?

    1   2   3   4   5   6   (7)   8   9   10

15. Do you have enough fun with your kids – or if you don't have kids, do you have enough play time?

    1   2   (3)   4   5   6   7   8   9   10

16. Do you have a habit of meeting new people?

     1   2   3   4   5   6   7   (8)   9   10

17. Do you feel positive about your future?

     1   2   3   4   5   6   7   8   (9)   10

18. Are you comfortable with the quality of your surroundings?

     1   2   3   4   5   6   7   8   9   (10)

19. Is taking care of your health a priority?

     1   2   3   4   5   6   7   8   9   (10)

20. Is the way you live your life a reflection of your values?

     1   2   3   4   5   6   7   8   9   (10)

Tally your score to find out where your love vibe is at:

180 – 200 - Love Vibe Superstar: You feel love all of the time, no matter what life throws at you. You radiate love and well being and others feel better just by being around you. Keep your daily love vibe practices going & remember to let others support you - or you know what happens, you could burn out and drop your love vibe.

155 – 179 - Love Vibe Rockstar: You are able to feel love most of the time. There is still room to supercharge your love vibe, so keep practicing and be sure to get the extra support you need!

100 -154 - Love Vibe Dancer: You are able to feel love sometimes and the good news is that you are on your way to feeling more love every day! Keep up your love vibe training practices and be sure to get the extra support you need.

Vibe Newbie: You are on your way to feeling more love! Keep on ~ing your love vibe and be sure to get the extra support you

Love Vibe Red Alert: Ok, I'm officially worried about you: It's time to ~w yourself to start feeling better. Go through this workbook again and participate fully in each training exercise. Be sure to get lots of professional support. Surround yourself with people that care about you. Do not go it alone, it is just too hard and you need an extra boost of energy to get you to supercharge your love vibe and feel better.

From your above answers you can clearly see which areas of your life you need to bring yourself into better centered alignment. This is a great indicator of where you need to supercharge your love vibe and take action to make changes. And always remember to get support!

Training Exercise 7-2

Need to supercharge your love Vibe Score or keep it high? Time to write out an action plan. Refer back to the exercises in this book and schedule time in your calendar to do the specific training exercises that will help you supercharge your love vibe in your low score areas. Need to take some bold outer world actions? Bring yourself to centered alignment, hear your own wisdom, get support, and Do It!!

Keep it going – do this course over and over again to supercharge your love vibe and gain the inner strength to make the outer world changes you deserve!!

Training Exercise 7-3

I'm having the best year of my life so far! Why? Because the first thing I do every morning is bring myself into centered alignment with my highest good. Remember how I used to align my energy with that of my imaginary romantic partner before getting out of bed and then one day he appeared? Well now I wake up every morning and the first thing I usually say to myself is, "I accept and love myself as I am. " That is a great way to stop judgments and mean trash talk before it even starts!

Then I affirm: "I center and align myself with my highest good and get everything done today that needs to get done." And I mean everything: exercise, eating well, work, serving my clients, meetings, socializing, which road to take… you name it. If it needs to get done IT DOES. If it didn't get done, IT OBVIOUSLY DIDN'T NEED TO HAPPEN. I repeat that mantra throughout the day to make sure I stay on track and listen to my body and inner needs, so that my highest good is always guiding me. Because my highest good knows better than I do - I'll skip meals and work myself into the ground unless I'm aligned first!

This trick allows me to be super productive, without burning myself out or being hard on myself. It allows me to respect my body and my relationship – because health and love come first for me! And yes, I still keep a successful career going, but not by sacrificing my health or my man. Now I trust that everything I do and everything I don't do is what needed to happen – and I let go of whatever I thought I "should" do. I stay strong and powerful throughout the whole work-day and have more fun, nourishment, and rest when I need it.

Another great alignment statement is, "I'm in the perfect place at the perfect time." I love that one, especially in all of this LA traffic.

Training Exercise 7-4

Want to know one of my little embarrassing secrets that really works to supercharge my love vibe? I'm a terrible singer and a goofy dancer, but if I sing a bouncy tune in my head or put on some music and shake my booty a bit – I FEEL SO MUCH BETTER IT IS AMAZING. As I am sitting here writing this workbook I am dancing in my seat. Yup, I'm all wiggly as I'm typing and I keep smiling because I don't really know the words to the song and I'm kind of butchering the tune and repeating the same part over again, but it is working to supercharge my love vibe, so I'm doing it!

And that is a key to healing. You've got to be WILLING to heal. You've got to be willing to look silly, feel happy for no reason, and let go of the baggage that has held you back for years. Just BE WILLING, COMMIT to doing your exercises, DO them, get SUPPORT, and you will supercharge your love vibe.

Here is a very personal, very extreme example of getting into centered alignment. I'm sharing it with you only because I intuit that some of you need to hear this level of my message to really get the importance of why centered alignment matters so much.

In the Spring of 2014 my neighbor had a violent outburst and my man and I suddenly decided to move out of our home. We didn't feel safe staying there, and even though we lived in an affordable apartment in the middle of our beloved neighborhood of Los Feliz, our safety came first and we had to leave.

We knew it was going to be stressful and we didn't want it to negatively impact our relationship, so we made a vow that we would not take out our fear or frustration on each other.

Even though we were utterly unprepared, we immediately rallied all of our friends and allies to pack our entire home and move out in just one day. We didn't know where we would end up and it was a very scary venture. But, we knew in our hearts that we were doing the right thing and that we would get through this together.

After we suddenly moved out, a generous kind friend gave us a place to stay while we were looking for a new home. 6 weeks later we were living in a new, luxury, huge, home at a price we could afford. We each had our own home office and felt incredibly grateful. AND, as fantastic as that apartment was and as in alignment as it was for us when we got it, we knew we would not be there long. We moved out after a year, but didn't find a new apartment in time and had to put everything in storage and spend the summer staying with awesome friends and subletting.

Sure, it was not convenient, but we knew we were in alignment with our next home and we just kept scouring the city and attracting it by vibrating at the frequency of us feeling happy in a home we love.

Now we live in the BEST home we've ever had together! It is exactly where we wanted up in the hills, has a great view, spacious, high ceilings, 2 fire places, a Jacuzzi tub, and we can walk to restaurants right down the street. We love it here! And, due to changing circumstances, we may have to move again next year, but we are staying in centered alignment and grateful for each wonderful home that comes our way.

Here is the secret truth I'm going to reveal to you, we hadn't been in alignment with that first Los Feliz apartment for a long time. We LOVED the location and the price and we were full of gratitude to be able to live there, that is why we stayed so long, but the quality of the building and management was very low and there wasn't enough space for us to comfortably live and work. It didn't match our love, money, or health vibe to stay living there nor did it match our centered alignment.

When you are not in alignment with your highest good, something always comes along and happens to try to FORCE YOU into alignment with your highest good. That most often happens in a disruptive way.

Over the last 23 years of helping people heal I have seen something happen over and over again; when people do not take good enough care of their health and well being, they often get sick or injured to a point that forces them to stay in bed and receive care. If they are stuck in a rut with finances, a traumatic unexpected expense happens. Or if they are out of alignment with their love life, a sudden upset or break up occurs. Can you think of a time when any of those ever happened to you? Is it happening to you now? Maybe you didn't recognize it as such until you got through this course, but I bet now you can see the link between what is going on in your life, the vibrations you are giving off, and whether or not you are in centered alignment!

Centered Alignment first allows you to infuse Love into every area of your life and see the abundance of love that is all around you.

CHAPTER 8 - ROUND UP

We live in deeds, not years; in thoughts, not breaths;

In feelings, not in figures on a dial.

We should count time by heart-throbs.

He most lives who thinks most—

feels the noblest—acts the best.

— Philip James Bailey

If you want to feel loving and energized, then regularly practice everything you learned throughout this Supercharge Your Love Vibe training. Don't stop. Do an exercise every day – I do! That is how I keep supercharging my love vibe!

Let's take stock of how you have already begun to supercharge your love vibe:

1. You've shifted love beliefs that were holding you back and your thoughts are now loving and kind.

2. You understand that needs are natural.

3. You value your own self worth.

4. You've made amends and are willing to forgive yourself.

5. You've opened the flow of giving and receiving.

6. You've gained love for your body.

7. You've activated your inner love magnet and can attract true love to you.

8. You speak words of love to yourself and others.

9. You've shifted to an attitude of gratitude.

10.   You allow yourself to feel love now.

11.   You've gotten into centered alignment.

12.   You've scheduled a Love Vibe action plan in your calendar!

These are the issues I had to deal with to open up my love channels and I continue to improve. What's amazing is that up until a few short years ago, I thought I might never be able to love a man again or be able to truly love myself. I've learned that the more love I notice all around me and let myself feel, the stronger my healing capabilities have become, and the more I can help others to heal.

My love vibe keeps improving steadily over time and shows itself in all kinds of ways.

• I have so much fun with my man and feel like I keep getting better at expressing my love for him. Even after 7.5 years the sex keeps getting better!

• I eat mostly organic healthy food and exercise regularly.

• I live in a wonderful home and you can feel the love when you walk through the front door.

• I have a dependable car, instead of the old clunker I suffered with for years.

• I keep improving my mind with continued education.

• I get massages, acupuncture, therapy, pedicures, healings and chiropractic care to express my love for my body & mind.

• I have the most amazing friends that I adore.

• I've let go of people and things that weren't loving me back.

• I'm so overflowing with love that I attract wonderful clients and feel excited to go to work each day.

Look back to exercise #1. How have those things on your list improved? Don't be hard on yourself if they haven't improved as much as you want them to YET. That just shows that you need to keep practicing supercharging your love vibe. Sometimes it takes hours and sometimes years to be able to sustain certain energy frequencies. Remember, it took me 2 years to get my love vibe strong enough for this awesome relationship I'm now in!

And remember, you don't have to go it alone.

I see so many people struggle by either trying to do everything all by themselves, or by thinking they can't stand on their own two feet. Both ends of that spectrum are painful! If you were meant to go it alone, there would only be one person walking the planet. So, never feel ashamed if you need help. You deserve to get the support that you truly need to transform your life in every way you want.

The Happy Woman Academy is full of generous caring women who have so much love to give, always feel free to reach out and ask for help. We love being here for each other, including YOU! We'll give you support, motivation, and accountability in supercharging your money, love, and health vibe. Just connect with www.TheHappyWomanAcademy.com to see when our next virtual course and live event or party is.

Let's all keep practicing supercharging our love vibe together so we can keep supercharging the conscious awareness on our planet and help everybody to feel the love they deserve.

I'm so proud of you for making it through this course and I sincerely hope that you keep practicing because I know how well it worked for me, my clients, and it will work for you. I look forward to hearing the great stories of how you have supercharged your love vibe!

With Love, Elizabeth

ALSO BY ELIZABETH MENZEL

Supercharge Your Health Vibe!

WOMEN'S HEALTH BEST-SELLER

Get ready to learn my favorite ways I keep my energy strong all day long, feel healthy even when I'm sick or injured, and how I learned to love my body and become the healthiest me I can be, so that you can do the same for yourself.

Supercharge Your Money Vibe!

WOMEN'S HEALTH BEST-SELLER

Get ready to learn the exact ways I quadrupled my financial income by changing my poverty consciousness to prosperity consciousness as well as how I improved my relationship with money – all while keeping my integrity and working less hours - so that you can do the same for yourself.

The 10-Minute Memoir

BEST-SELLER

This book came from a deep heartfelt desire to know the stories of my family. Write Your Memoir In Just 10 Minutes A Day With This Easy Q&A Journal

ABOUT ELIZABETH

Elizabeth Menzel is a certified Brennan Healing Science practitioner and serves as a speaker, best selling author, Happy Woman Mentor, and she's the founder of the award winning Happy Woman Academy. Her books and programs focus on ending the cycle of sacrifice, sabotage, and neglect so that women can enjoy massive success in their career, health, and love life.

She uses proven neuroscience and physics based healing systems and has facilitated thousands of transformations over the last 23 years. Her live events & Happiness Training Programs teach busy women of all ages powerful "on the go" ways to heal their body, invigorate their romance, and boost their career – so they can receive more money while enjoying life more fully! She's on a mission to teach 1,000,000 women "The Happy Woman Formula" by 2020.

The mission of the Happy Woman Academy is to provide women with a safe and sacred space to learn how to easily receive more love, health, and money by using proven science based healing systems and the power of communion and laughter.

The vision of the Happy Woman Academy is to restore the Feminine to her rightful place of honor & value next to the Masculine in society, thereby restoring harmonic balance to humanity, the earth, & nature. Big vision I know, but it's the one I've got.

CONNECT WITH ME

Visit www.TheHappyWomanAcademy.com/quiz

And take the 30 second quiz to find out the

#1 way you Sabotage Your Success & Happiness

AND

Visit the Happy Woman Academy on Facebook at

https://www.facebook.com/TheHappyWomanAcademy/

AND

If you'd like 1-1 mentorship with me,

you can apply for a Best Next Step Call @

bit.ly/bestnextstep

AND

I love hearing from my readers, so please feel free to

leave a positive review on my Amazon Author page

at bit.ly/AmazonAuthorElizabethMenzel

If you are a man, get in on the transformational community you need here: DaleThomasVaughn.com.

Photos by Ken Morris (Glitch.photography) and Eric Beteille (PedestrianPhotographer.com).

BIBLIOGRAPHY

1 Wijk, Roeland Van. "An Introduction to Human Biophoton Emission." National Center for Biotechnology Information. U.S. National Library of Medicine, 12 Apr. 2005. Web. 21 Mar. 2015.

2 William Walker Atkinson. Thought Vibration or the Law of Attraction. Advanced Thought Publishing. 1906

3 Tan, Enoch. "Secrets of Mind and Reality." Nature of Vibration in the Spiritual Dimension. MindReality.com. Web. 21 Mar. 2015.

4 Bergeisen, Michael. "The Neuroscience of Happiness." The Neuroscience of Happiness. Berkeley College, 22 Sept. 2010. Web. 21 Mar. 2015. Journal of Homosexuality, Vol. 45(1) 2003

5 Turner, Ashley. "How Meditation Changes Your Brain Frequency." MindBodyGreen. MindBodyGreen.com, 5 Feb. 2014. Web. 21 Mar. 2015.

6 Lagopoulos et al. Increased Theta and Alpha EEG Activity During Nondirective Meditation. The Journal of Alternative and Complementary Medicine, 2009; 15 (11): 1187 DOI: 10.1089/acm.2009.0113

7 Turner, Ashley. "How Meditation Changes Your Brain Frequency." *MindBodyGreen*. MindBodyGreen.com, 5 Feb. 2014. Web. 21 Mar. 2015.

8 Lagopoulos et al. Increased Theta and Alpha EEG Activity During Nondirective Meditation. The Journal of Alternative and Complementary Medicine, 2009; 15 (11): 1187 DOI: 10.1089/acm.2009.0113

9 Hurley, Dan. "Grandma's Experiences Leave a Mark on Your Genes." Discover Magazine. DiscoverMagazine.com, 11 June 2013. Web. 21 Mar. 2015.
Nature Neuroscience 7, 847 - 854 (2004)

10 Jornal de Pediatria - Vol. 80, No.2(Suppl), 2004

11 The Journal of Neuroscience, 7 June 2006, 26(23): 6314-6317

12 Szalavitz, Maia. "Reality Check: Why Some Brains Can't Tell Real From Imagined | TIME.com." Time.com. Time, 5 Oct. 2011. Web. 21 Mar. 2015.

13 The Journal of Neuroscience, October 5, 2011 31(40):14308-14313

Made in United States
Orlando, FL
15 March 2022

15784662R00052